BRYAN ALEC FLOYD was born and reared in Oklahoma. He graduated from Seattle University in 1966. The following two years he served in the Marine Corps, and on release from service, he taught English in high schools and colleges in the Washington and Maryland areas for four years. He received a masters degree in 1974 from Johns Hopkins University. He now lives on Long Island, where he teaches at Suffolk County Community College and is at work on a group of short stories.

THE
LONG WAR DEAD:
AN EPIPHANY
1st Platoon, U.S.M.C.

BRYAN ALEC FLOYD

A BARD BOOK/PUBLISHED BY AVON BOOKS

THE LONG WAR DEAD: AN EPIPHANY is an original publication of Avon Books. Published in a Bard format, it has never appeared in book form.

AVON BOOKS
A division of
The Hearst Corporation
959 Eighth Avenue
New York, New York 10019

ISBN: 0-380-00524-7

First Bard Printing, February, 1976

BARD TRADEMARK REG. U.S. PAT. OFF. AND
FOREIGN COUNTRIES, REGISTERED TRADEMARK—
MARCA REGISTRADA, HECHO EN CHICAGO, U.S.A.

Printed in the U.S.A.

To Aleksandr Solzhenitsyn
To Colonel Anthony Herbert, U.S. Army
To Colonel William Corson, U.S. Marine Corps
And lastly, to the men who helped me fight the
good fight against the enemy.

The author extends much gratitude to the following people:
Robert Harmon, Ralph, Polly, Ken, Carol, Jane Bloom, Fr.
Costello, Fr. Toulouse, Fr. Nigro, Mack Scism, Jean and
Henry Munde, Dr. Guppy, Dr. Hurley, Janice Howell, Julie
Parvin, Dave Parvin, Peter Olwell, Pat and Marissa Beaton,
Fr. Bartnick, Fr. Donavan, Ted and Mrs. Bennett, Gene
Langford, Mr. and Mrs. John Troxler, Mary Beth Celio, Pat
Silvernails, the Hopkins people who did their homework,
Elliott, Steve, Mary, Hal, Scott, Hal, Bernie, Harlan, Patty,
Eric, and my wife Nancy and our son Ian, who both are
poems.

There were men who opposed the invasion or at the very least were uneasy with it, and to a degree, they were the same men who would later oppose the Vietnam commitment. One was General David M. Shoup, Commandant of the Marine Corps. When talk about invading Cuba was becoming fashionable, General Shoup did a remarkable display with maps. First he took an overlay of Cuba and placed it over the map of the United States. To everybody's surprise, Cuba was not a small island along the lines of, say, Long Island, at best. It was about 800 miles long and seemed to stretch from New York to Chicago. Then he took another overlay, with a red dot, and placed it over the map of Cuba. "What's that?" someone asked him. "That, gentlemen, represents the size of the island of Tarawa," said Shoup, who had won a Medal of Honor there, "and it took us three days and eighteen thousand Marines to take it."

—David Halberstam
The Best and the Brightest

Carrying his remaining two bombs, he had dived that Handly-Page at the château where the generals sat at lunch, until McGinnis, at the toggles below him, began to shout at him, before he ever signaled. He didn't signal until he could discern separately the slate tiles of the roof. Then his hand dropped and he zoomed, and he held the aeroplane so, in its wild snarl, his lips parted, his breath hissing, thinking: "God! God! If they were all there—all the generals, the admirals, the presidents, and the kings—theirs, ours—all of them."

—William Faulkner
Turnabout

They wrote in the old days that it is sweet and fitting to die for one's country. But in modern war there is nothing sweet nor fitting in your dying. You will die like a dog for no good reason.

The world is a fine place and worth fighting for.

—Ernest Hemingway
Notes on the Next War
and
For Whom the Bell Tolls

I don't mind fighting communists or fascists. They're all and everyone of the bastards sonsabitches. But I don't want to fight them with the Pentagon tying one hand behind my back while the politicians have me by the balls. If the V.C. or the North Viets fight like Indians, let us fight like Indians, too. Hell, we are Indians. If the Reds want a weird battle in a weird war, then right on. When General Chesty Puller and his Marines were totally encircled by the Communists in Korea, he simply said, "The poor bastards: they've got us surrounded," and the Marines literally exterminated the best crack troops the Chinese had. In this war, we're now told we are surrounded and we're ordered to hold. Hold? Hold for what, man? We're Marines. Our entire training is to kill the enemy while he's holding, then move the fuck out.
——A Marine PFC at Khe Sahn

Contents

Corporal Curt Meadows, U.S.M.C.

In the warp of military time,
his father got his son's last letter
after he had received
official word of his son's death.
His son's letter read:
"And there will be old memories
made alive and young
of the dying and the dead
the living have no right to forget."

Private Ian Godwin, U.S.M.C.

He stepped on a land mine,
falling up instead of down.
Afterward he lay still, listening
to his feet get up without him
and slowly walk away.
For this he was given a medal,
which he swallowed.
He was given crutches,
which he burned.
Flown Med-Evac to San Diego,
he was ordered to rehabilitate.
But he started to salute bedpans
and give orders to hypos,
and tell catheters to "Fire!"
He stood on his stumps,
yelling that he was going
to chase daisies up the hills
because winter had greened into spring,
that God had become rain and it was raining,
the soft mud of Vietnam cool between his toes.

Sergeant Brandon Just, U.S.M.C.

He was alive with death:
Her name was Sung
and she was six years old.
By slightest mistake of degrees
on an artillery azimuth,
he had called for rockets and napalm.
Their wild wizardry of firepower
expired her mistake of a village,
killing everyone except her,
and napalm made her look
like she was dead among the dead,
she alone alive among their upturned corpses
burning toward the sky.
He and the platoon
got to them too late,
removing only her
to a hospital inside his base, Da Nang.
In the months that followed,
when he could make it back from the boonies,
he always went to visit Sung.
Finally he was ordered to a desk job at the base.
He visited her every day,
though he accused himself of being alive
and would stand in a slump,

breathing his despair,
before entering the children's ward.
But he would enter.
Sung, knowing it was him,
would turn toward the sound of his feet,
her own, seared beyond being feet,
crisply trying to stand on shadows,
cool but unseen.
And as he would come in,
Sung would hobble up to him
in her therapeutic cart,
smiling even when she did not smile, lipless,
her chin melted to her chest
that would never become breasts.
He would stand
and wait for her touch upon his hand
with her burn-splayed fingers
that came to lay a fire upon his flesh.
Sung was alive
and would live on despite life,
but even now her skull
seemed to be working its way through
the thin, fragile solids of wasted, waxen skin.
Her head was as bald as a bomb
whose paint had peeled.

She had no nose
and her ears were gone.
Her eyes had been removed,
and because they were not there,
they were there
invisibly looking him through.
Sung was child-happy
that he came and cared,
and when he would start to leave,
she would agonize her words
out of the hollow that was her mouth.
Her tongue, bitten in two while she had burned,
strafing his ears,
saying, without mercy,
I love you.

Corporal Charles Chungtu, U.S.M.C.

This is what the war ended up being about:
we would find a V.C. village,
and if we could not capture it
or clear it of Cong,
we called for jets.
The jets would come in, low and terrible,
sweeping down, and screaming,
in their first pass over the village.
Then they would return, dropping their first bombs
that flattened the huts to rubble and debris.
And then the jets would sweep back again
and drop more bombs
that blew the rubble and debris
to dust and ashes.
And then the jets would come back once again,
in a last pass, this time to drop napalm
that burned the dust and ashes to just nothing.
Then the village
that was not a village any more
was our village.

Private Rex Jones, U.S.M.C.

Eighteen years old
and wild for war,
he volunteered.
After two weeks in Nam
he defined Eternity as a tour of duty:
thirteen months.
He was a born loser,
ghetto-born and raised,
a high school drop-out and finally a grunt,
but he defined *Forever*.
His definition was so utterly simple
even the Pentagon physicists
understood it.
When old Rex bought the farm
and was a hero,
he was buried in Arlington,
not far from the Kennedy brothers.
He joined half of his platoon there.
Several of us who came back
visited old Rex,
thinking we would say something.
None of us said a word.
Eighteen years old.

BRYAN ALEC FLOYD

Private Jesus Santiago, U.S.M.C.

Directive: NAVAL 1842639-WIA *Date:* 20 Feb 76

To: Lt Cmdr Marshall Tipper, USN
Ass't Neurosurgeon
San Francisco Naval Hospital

From: Cmdr Trevor Hartwright, USN
Neurosurgeon
Asaki, Japan

Subj: USMC Pvt Santiago, Jesus

He lost
his maxillary sinuses,
both mandibles,
both eyes,
and both frontal lobes of his brain,
which has somewhat dulled his reactions
to these traumas.
He is mentally subdued
and less aware of his deficits
than otherwise he would be
if he had not undergone a lobotomy
from bullet shrapnel, type AK47

———————————

(patient was prisoner of war of North Vietnamese
but due to rank and ignorance
was supposedly disposed of
and left as being expired).
Infection and continued leaking
of spinal fluid
have caused certain vicissitudes:
he might have a paralyzed limb,
or two or three or four.
Due to these negations
if patient does again become "aware"
he will be unable to speak,
reason, protest, or assent,
becoming a kind of silent minority.
Other morbid complications include
having to lie face down or on his side
forever
so that he will not aspirate
into his lungs any excess, unwanted secretions,
like vomit,
which would make his situation precarious.
Being comotose,
he is not cognizant of his obligation
to empty his bladder
or evacuate his bowels, voluntarily,

and therefore will need a constant catheter
and daily/nightly enemas.
Parts of him
keep becoming necrotic,
necessitating surgical excise.
Personnel should be aware of this issue.
For the present and future
eliminate any requisite
of need for cosmetic surgery.

Lance Corporal Purdue Grace, U.S.M.C.

He went home when the new replacements
    arrived,
but before he left
he talked with several of them,
all of whom looked scared and a bit self-pitying.
They knew he had made it through his tour
without getting a cold much less a wound.
One of the braver replacements
told him they were all terrified.
The Lance Corporal told them, "To be scared is
    okay.
I've seen lots of men change their pants
more than once a day, they were so scared.
But don't expect sympathy.
Sympathy is a sad word found in the dictionary
somewhere between scab and syphilis.
Always remember to keep your head out of your
    ass
and your ass out of the air.
Know this about this fucked-up war
that will never unfuck itself—
Life in Vietnam is a sea of shit:
Some people sink.
Some people swim.
And some people go in boats."

Private Joseph Plainview, U.S.M.C.

M.I.A.

Lance Corporal Frank Realf, U.S.M.C.

After we would come back from the boonies
and before being allowed on leave
we would sometimes be shown films
on gonorrhea and syphilis.
The films would always be in blazing movie color
which was graphic
and supposed to encourage us
to stay clear of the B-girls
in Mama San Portia's in Da Nang
or the sweet tricks
in Diamond Lou's in Saigon.
But instead, the films always
made us horny
because they were in movie color and were
    graphic.
Besides, a man with the drips
couldn't be sent back into combat.
Rumor had it
that if anyone caught one of the diseases,
the enlisted Marines would give him a hundred
    bucks.
Rumor also had it
that if a man got both diseases,
he'd become a millionaire.

First Lieutenant Royal Young, U.S.M.C.

The Lieutenant said
he hoped to fall a corpse if he was lying,
swearing he had seen Christ
humping it in the paddies with the refugees.
The platoon thought
the sun had gotten into his head
and had done something to the Lieutenant's eyes.
He stood there, more air than flesh,
under a sun that was bleeding down,
and grinned through his sobs.
The Gunnery Sergeant told the platoon to take five.
"Gunny Sergeant!" someone screamed.
Everyone flattened.
But it was no mortar or rocket round.
Everyone looked up.
The Lieutenant was still standing,
both of his eyes plucked out,
the sockets staring
hollow and bleeding,
his bayonet, gouted, at his feet.
We kept him alive.

Corporal Norman Callows, U.S.M.C.

As if by some strange agreement
with some strange hell,
he said that doing people a hurt rested him.
The way he tells it,
he used to be a sonofabitch,
and really used to worry about it,
but since he was sent to Vietnam
and then was found guilty
of murdering six women and their nine children.
He just doesn't worry about it.

Corporal Victor Vanderbilt, U.S.M.C.

After the Marines liberated Hue
they dug up the bodies
the Viet Cong left behind,
the three thousand corpses who, when alive,
refused or were unable to rise
to ever higher and higher levels
of political consciousness,
and so were beaten and hacked and shot
to death after death after death,
liberated by their own.
The Marines thought
they had seen everything,
but nothing had ever been like this.
He went to a couple
who were on their knees, the tiny remains
of their year-old child before them.
Their baby had not lived long enough
to hate the world
or to blame life its living death called war.
Its mother was silent
beyond all silence;
its father dead
beyond all death.
Yet she spoke, sobbing.

Yet he breathed, wailing.
Their child had left them
listening to the song of shrapnel
when a bullet pierced its ears and brain.
It was so young
it had looked at everything,
understanding nothing.
Except its mother.
Except its father.
They were alive
and they were dead.

_____

Unknown, U.S.M.C.

Anything that needs a lie is itself false.
This war, like all wars,
needed several lies.
Even the liars believed the lies.
When some of the Senators
told the President he was lying,
The President did not believe them.
When some of the Colonels
told the Generals that the Generals were lying,
the Generals did not believe them.
Many politicians,
who thought caution cowardice,
did not confine their thoughts
to mere reason,
and so controlled most Generals
by obeying them.
If anything in this war
is to be learned
it is this: most Generals are politicians
in uniform.
Yet I forgive them.
They are not worth my hatred.
I know who they are
because I know who I am.

But because they do not know
what they are
they will never know me,
they with their plans and operations and missions.
The leaders on both sides wanted facts,
so they got facts,
and in the getting of facts,
did away with reality.
Each side knew
that life is not longitude,
but neither knew
that death is only one denouement:
those of us who died, *died*,
but we will have to die again:
we will be forgotten.

Private Jack Smith, U.S.M.C.

Since he came back
he never met with the friends he fought with in
  Nam
and never mentioned the war:
Once he was ordered out
of his five-man fire team
to go and be point man.
He was about a hundred feet up front
when someone in his fire team
tripped a land mine,
and whoever it had been,
along with the other three,
were left somehow
unreasonably alive—just.
And there had been a Lance Corporal in his squad
whom the threat of peace always made aggressive.
The Lance Corporal was a sniper
with twenty-six kills marked up.
The Private was with him
when the Lance Corporal was cut down by a V.C.
  sniper,
and as the Private held him,

the Lance Corporal held his intestines in his hands,
saying, "I don't want to die. I'm afraid to die."
And died.
One night the Private and two other guys
slept in a sandbagged hootch
that was hit by two direct mortar rounds,
he being blasted awake and away
without a scratch
while those other two
were just pieces of themselves.
He could not find their heads
but laid the rest to rest
in ponchos that no one could tag
because their remains were Officially Unidentifiable.
After that he decided
to avoid moderation at any extreme
and shot every anything that moved.
He came to think that his officers
were more concerned with rank and medals
than with the lives and deaths of their men.
He came to feel that his politicians were garbage
who should have been wasted.
When he finished his tour of duty
and was sent home and Honorably Discharged,
he decided to live with his parents
and began college,

and majored in History on the GI Bill.
He thought he might join the peace movement
and started going to rallies.
His college was shut down four times
the semester he started,
and during the fourth shutdown,
his college president was beaten up
by several anti-imperialists
who took over the college
and burned down the ROTC building
and the library
and who kept the president in his office
until he resigned, on his own accord of course.
But the ex-Private kept going to the rallies,
looked, listened, learned.
He got to thinking
that most of the rally speakers
were happy with hallucinations,
and he thought
that several of the tens of thousands
in the crowds who kept yelling Right On
had either forgotten, or had never known,
that absolutism is addictive
and that the mob, any mob for any cause,
is always
pregnant with fascism.

The fifth time his college was shut down
by the anti-imperialist anti-
fascists,
he knew what he knew,
and knew that he must try
to walk through and beyond the mob
which had blocked his way to History.
He tried, knowing they would beat hell out of
    him,
and they did.
But it was he who was arrested
for disturbing the peace.
He was jailed.
His dad bailed him out
and told him he hoped he was satisfied
and that he should have felt ashamed.
But instead, the ex-Private felt himself feel
    nothing.
He went home again, and packed, and left.
That was four years ago.
Nobody has heard from him since.

Private First Class Cassidy Gavin, U.S.M.C.

His face always broke pale
at the sight of dead children,
their deaths brought about
mostly by bombs,
often from a fire fight,
and sometimes by torture.
He said of such deaths
that they were done
by people who were less than human.
For those first few months in Nam,
he tried to turn off the killing—
and the killing of his soul.
He went down through those days
trying to numb himself against himself.
Because he breathed
and was conscious of it,
he knew he was alive.
But after a while,
the war and its dead children
became so sick and sickening
he could no longer even try to turn it off.
On his first R & R in Bangkok,
he shot himself up with sweet smack heroin

and watched his hands go calm.
From then on out
he carried it with him
back into the boonies.
And it was not long before he knew he was dead
even before he died,
but he did not mind.
The shadows of the jungle began to shine
and he could hear the wild flowers
talking their colors.
He was on a fine high
when he finally got hit,
the bullet from somewhere
singing into his heart.
He fell, and his falling felt heavy and light at once,
and for a moment of a second he was afraid.
His falling went on
for longer than he could tell,
the shell inside him only slowly searching for a
    way out,
but just as he hit earth,
all fear fell with him.
He lay still and smiled at God
and let himself sink
into a relaxing, bloodless depression
while he listened to the dead children call his name.

35

Corporal Myron Striker, U.S.M.C.

You didn't realize how good you were
at killing
until afterward when,
say with a four or five body-count to your credit,
you thought about it because you had time
to realize how simply it had been done,
say in about ten to fifteen seconds,
and that nothing had been sloppy or clumsy.
Except for the thumpthumpthump
of your rifle on automatic,
it was quiet, even when they fell,
their falling noiseless
as if they did not want
to spoil the silence of their death.
You and your squad were usually kneeling
or in a belly position during an ambush.
Even your sweat seemed to hold back
in hushed patches.
You had recon'd this zone
and knew Charley was coming
(always) in a small party,
six to twelve at most,
coming pointless.
You waited until

they were right there—
all but upon you—and then
you just thumpthumped them to death
and heaved a grenade into the bodies,
just to make certain
there was no motion left
except your motion.
You weren't aware of all this
until you moved.
Then, for a second,
you thought about it.

Private First Class George Rooney, U.S.M.C.

Like a second brain inside his skull,
his panic outran his reason
and his body followed his panic.
He took perhaps three steps
before the hunting, haunting machine-gun fire
harrowed a cross upon his back,
turned him around,
and kept him from dropping
by dozens of bursts into his belly
that bounced him up and down
in an insane, obscene dance
that went on and on and on.
Then the firing stopped.
His legs rubbered down
as he sat in a cross-legged squat
and said, "Oh?"
Then nothing.

Lance Corporal Elmer Rodin, U.S.M.C.

He was a grenadier and a genius with a machine
    gun,
and he laughed forever
at the Marine Corps, the North Vietnamese,
the peace movement, himself.
He was wounded twice,
each time receiving only a few tiny fragments
of shrapnel in his rump,
which he said made him both half-witted and
    half-assed.
He claimed if he received another wound in his
    butt
he was going to write Hanoi
and tell them that the Viet Cong
took this war too seriously.
He said his greatest desire in life
was to someday possess
the known intelligence of a Comrade Tom
    Hayden,
the sensitive honesty of a Senator Joe McCarthy,
the political acumen of a Ms. Joan Baez,
and the racial equality of a Herr Lincoln Rockwell,
and that with these world famous attributes,
he would run for Premier or President

39

so that mankind would build a statue of him
that would forever stand tall and bold
and shat upon.
On the day he was going home,
he said he was terribly worried
about the one problem in his life.
This problem, he said,
consisted in having to choose between two women
who were waiting for him back in the States
to come home a hero and marry one of them.
The difficulty was this:
one woman kept her legs so tight together
he swore to God she only had one foot,
while the other woman had been had so many
    times
he knew for a fact that she was using her cherry
    as a taillight.
Some women, he said.
Some choice.

Private Nels Larson-Berman, U.S.M.C.

Sometimes he thinks he is only a thought of
    himself,
that he and all of those who are around him
do not really exist.
He has been back home now for three years.
You would think his mind
would have dipped and drained itself
of the war by now
in time's own flushing.
But he is always alone,
and even himself seems too much company for
    him.
Back into college again,
he attends classes
with a mixture of dread and boredom.
He has not declared a major
and does not know what he wants to be.
In his Psychology class recently,
the professor, who knew the former Private was a
    Viet vet,
asked him to relate the difficulty
many veterans were having
in adjusting to civilian life.

He opened his mouth
but stayed silent.
His eyes looked all around the room,
and his eyes cracked and shattered and melted like
    ice.

Private First Class Miro Cayey, U.S.M.C.

He started talking about crosses and crucifixes
right after Operation Crossbow was finished.
He kept telling everyone
that he was seeing crosses everywhere,
even when they were not there:
in telephone poles, window frames, trees,
cracks in the dust and mud and pavement,
the creases of his palms,
as if he had crucifixes in his very eyeballs.
Guys would be talking to him about anything—
women, cars, home, sports—
and he would start to talk about God and crosses,
saying out of nowhere,
"Is God an inkblot?"
"When did Christ find out he was God?"
"What if God treated people
like people treat him?"
"If there is a hell,
and if God is everywhere,
is God in hell?"
Men in the platoon, especially in his squad,
started to avoid him.
He didn't seem to mind.
After each mission,

he would just start over again,
asking those questions of his.
The day the platoon heard
that a Corporal in the company
had wasted over a dozen women and children
just to watch them die
and then had buried them in a ditch,
the PFC was ordered to go with his fire-team
and dig up the corpses.
He followed his orders,
and when the corpses were laid out in a row
above the ditch,
a Private later said that the PFC started to act
    funny,
that he got down into the ditch and looked up
at the men who had helped him dig up the corpses
and that then the PFC said, "Is there a God?"
Then he took his rifle,
put the barrel into his mouth,
pulled the trigger,
blew his head off,
and found out.

Private First Class David Princeton, U.S.M.C.

It took ten days for him to die.
Gangrene set in right after he was hit.
The gangrene killed the lower half of him
during the first five days.
He told the doctors,
after they told him he was going to die,
to never be guilty of innocence.
Then he waited for the rest to die
and told the hospital Chaplain
that when death came
it would be as if the earth would tilt
and he would fall off, and falling,
would again stand tall and whole.
He said that then he would come back
and chase down the meaning of his death
and kill it
so that he could stay dead.
He died sometime in the night.
When they found him the next morning,
he was on the floor,
having fallen out of bed.

Corporal Ben Mann, U.S.M.C.

In the stilled air and swirling heat for hours
we had not made to move, waiting.
Then there came down a gust of wind,
just one and at that a short one,
yet one was enough to tell that others,
longer, were coming.
Down from out the sky
whispered a din, a faint rain,
merely a whisper
and hardly a din at all.
We were down behind bushes
and faced a flank of thick trees
that were about a hundred yards away.
Nothing was in sight
but the grass and the sky.
Then, they started coming slowly out of the trees.
One of them seemed to be taking his way alone,
looking this way, far over here
where his eyes were led to look
but not to see
me, alone; as I looked at him, alone;
he, my first.

And I commenced to cry, quietly.
Quietly: they—closer; then—close,
and not seeing
as I opened up on him,
his face fading
when my firing disappeared his eyes
and my bullets nudged his brain
out of the back of his skull,
he falling forever,
leaving me alive and full,
never to be empty of his eyes.

Private 2147652, U.S.M.C.

The Commander-in-Chief
The President of the United States of America
1600 Pennsylvania Avenue
Washington, D.C. 20500

20 Feb 1976

Sir:

During the Vietnam era
3,000,000 men
served in southeast Asia.
2,600,000 men
were disabled.
275,000 men
cannot today as veterans find jobs.
153,311 men
were wounded by nonhostile causes.
60,000 to 200,000 men
are Viet veterans who became and remain heroin
    addicts.
90,000 to 100,000 men
are today in V.A. hospitals.
46,097 men
were killed in action.
23,214 men

became one hundred percent totally disabled,
    physically.
13,167 men
became one hundred percent totally disabled,
    psychologically.
10,317 men
are dead from nonhostile causes.
1,500 men
were prisoners of war.
1,100 men
are M.I.A.
1 man, Private 2147652,
is unofficially in all
but two of the above—listed categories:
that of being killed in action
and that of being killed by nonhostile causes.
Because he lost his hands and feet,
and because he is addicted to heroin,
and because he has malaria,
and because he has had a total physical collapse,
and because he has had a complete mental break-
    down,
and because his wife divorced him
because only part of him finally came home,
and because he has spent the past three years
in and out of jails and hospitals,

and because he won the Congressional Medal of
    Honor
which he hocked for a fix,
we, his physicians, are in a dilemma:
we consider him dead
but cannot figure out
which of the two catagories to put him in:
killed in action,
or dead from nonhostile causes.
Please reply by command.

Signed,
his physicians
Bethesda Naval Hospital
Bethesda, Maryland 20014

Captain James Leson, U.S.M.C.

His corpse was returned
to the U.S. in March, 1974, from Hanoi,
where the criminal Captain had been
a prisoner from 1967 until his natural death in
   1973.
An official spokesman
of the Peoples' Republic of North Vietnam
related with regrets
that the bourgeois elitest officer
had confessed to having been a lackey
for the war-mongering capitalists
and their running dogs, the South Vietnamese.
The official spokesman said
the aristocratic officer, without being intimidated,
had confessed that he had enjoyed killing innocent
   children
and had loved watching cities and villages burn.
And that before the imperialist Captain had
   naturally died,
he had written his regrets and spoken them over
   the radio
that his sins and the sins of his mafia nation
could have been avoided

had he been as brave as a Rennie Davis or a
    Jane Fonda
and his country as committed to fighting
    inequality and racism
as the governments of Sweden and India.
Enough said,
he said before he died his natural death.

Lance Corporal Nathanial Hampshire, U.S.M.C.

Almost illiterate,
he had always been a success at failure,
but the Marine Corps accepted him
because they told him
the Corps was looking for a few good men.
He went to Vietnam as a grunt,
and when his death happened,
it happened needlessly,
a mishap of war, by simple mistake.
He had been out on night patrol
when he and his squad were ambushed.
Everyone died, except him.
He was shot through the throat
and managed to stumble and crawl his way back
to the friendly zone.
A Private who was standing night watch
heard a sound and waited for a friendly signal.
But the wounded man could not speak
and could no longer even stumble or crawl.
The Private opened up on him,
blowing him away.
Then the Private was ordered out
to go and see what was left of what he had done.

He came and knelt above the Lance Corporal
and took him up in his arms, rocked him back and
    forth,
saying, "I'm sorry, man.
Can you hear me, man?"
And the dead man said nothing,
and his silence spoke,
and even his silence was a wasted passion.

Private Lennon Pancake III, U.S.M.C.

Between operations,
if there were time,
we would get a few days off
from combat duty.
The Lieutenants and Sergeants would be called
   together
for what they referred to as The Lecture.
The Company Commander would tell them
that they had A Duty
and were not Being As Conscientious
as they Should Be
about Deep, Dark, and Dangerous Drugs like
   heroin.
And pot.
Then the Chaplain would preach to them
that they had A Leader's Moral Obligation
to Constantly Be On The Alert
against Communist-Controlled Narcotics like
   heroin.
And pot.
Then the Lieutenants and Sergeants would return
   to us,
pass around their pipes,
and tell us to stay away from heroin,

and we would be taking a toke from their pipes,
and say back to them in unison,
"And pot."

Private First Class Jefferson Lee, U.S.M.C.

No one knew
and no one could tell
if it had been mortars, rockets,
artillery, or land mines,
the earth was gouged and gutted from all of these.
When such a corpse
was among several such corpses
and they were in that condition
of damage and rot,
it was impossible to say,
not that it mattered to him or them
or to those whose job it was
to gather up the pieces
and put them into body bags.
Along with the others,
his remains were Officially Identified
by dog tag.
When shipped back for burial
in a sealed casket,
such corpses were named
with such exactitude,
truth about such matters
meaning being honest about such lies.

Corporal Kevin Spina, U.S.M.C.

He came of a sharecrop farm family
and could barely read and write.
He had never thought
about teaching his heart war.
When he personally received
a letter from the President
of the United States of America
he simply went, having faith.
He put on his uniform
and disappeared
and became his uniform.
When he came back in a box,
he was buried with full military honors,
his family given the flag
that draped his coffin.
Now that flag flies every day
in front of his house.
When the neighbors' children pass by
they always look at that flag
and they always say,
"Someday there will be another war,
and I'm going to be a Marine."

Sergeant Jules Beaumont, U.S.M.C.

He was who he was,
not what others thought him to be.
Even when people are two dimensional,
they are not two dimensional.
He was a lifer,
a professional Marine,
a former Drill Instructor,
and a posthumous winner
of the Congressional Medal of Honor.
He hated nothing and no one.
He had his doubts and disbeliefs about the war
and did not swallow everything his politicians said.
He was no flag-waver
nor a defender of capitalism,
and he did not believe
that the Marine Corps was here before God.
Had his superiors told him that salt was sweet
he would not have called salt sugar.
He was what he was: a lifer, a Marine, a D.I.
Yet he cared little about medals,
thought warfare absurd,
and officers made him smile,
especially Second Lieutenants and Generals.
Most of his friends were civilians.

He was, like many professional military men,
a stranger who stayed the stranger
to the officers above him
and to the enlisted men below.
Just before his platoon was sent out
on Operation Hastings, where he died,
he gave to the Chaplain his own epitaph,
which today is written on a small rock slab
that marks his grave in Arlington:
"For those of us who fought and died for them,
Peace and Freedom have a flavor
that fascists and communists
will never know."

Private First Class Brooks Morgenstein, U.S.M.C.

Her remembered frailty had strengthened his.
His soul was alive for her.
What kept him going
when he would bag and tag bodies
or when out on a search-and-destroy
were her eyes as soft as breasts.
He wanted to write his wife naked words
that would have been more naked when read.
He had chosen the goal of his groin
and it was to grieve,
for his want of her was like pain.
His loneliness and lust were his and he theirs
during every second of these thirteen months.
He only knew as he held his rifle
during a sweeping operation
that next year he would hold her,
and when he kissed her,
his tongue would touch hers
and she would feel
as though a piece of the sun
was in her mouth.
When someone in his platoon
was sent back in pieces, alive or dead,

he tried not to despair of heaven,
but sometimes he had faith only in flesh
and would think of her thighs
and remember God.
The heat of the jungle
had pared him thin as peace.
His head was shaven squabby bald.
His uniform clung to him like a huge wet sock,
and he stank of leeches and mud and malaria and
    fear.
Yet he was all he had,
and his heart would leave him, and long to her
    heart,
she who had been shy to yield, but had yielded.
The sun in the boonies gloomed everything
with its yellowed heat for air,
but he breathed her fingers.
And her young woman's youngest breasts
suckled his terror,
while her mouth held off boredom
from shattering him insane.
Under a rocket barrage at Khe Sahn,
he once dreamed of her lying open as a wound,
and as raw,
and he had salved and bandaged her
with his mouth and fingers.

During the bad times,
such as when the platoon was ordered to torch a
    village,
he would feel his rage deepening,
without bottoming out,
and he would be shaking with fear and shame and
    ecstasy
that he was still alive.
He would make himself think of her,
and with the thirst that comes from drinking of it,
his lust would grow and become exalted
like a great tree,
and he knew if he made it back
she could climb his body
and that he with branches would cover her with
    himself
and they would be unable to tell
how much of him was him
and how much of him was her.

Private First Class Sy Converse, U.S.M.C.

He thought so much death
could never stay dead.
When told the rumor
that the truce was near
to being signed in Paris,
he felt the end would never end.
In those last days, waiting,
his breathing soothed him,
by its mere coming in,
its mere going out.
In the night before the day the firing ceased,
he was on guard duty,
hoping this night would come to a quick close,
for the night belonged to the V.C.
He was crouched next to a Corporal
when he felt a sharp tickle in his chest and heart
and felt the tickle laugh up
from his heart to his brain.
He stood up and said,
"Am I dead?"
and fell,
and was.

Lance Corporal Hunter Ward, U.S.M.C.

When he returned from war's reality
to the unreality of peace
and became a civilian again,
his life seemed to have no meaning,
though his death was no longer necessary.
Breathing bloodless aspirations,
he frailly footed it
from one unhiring job to another
and finally found one that paid something.
And so with his peace-numbed brain
then flunked his way through college,
feeling like a worm in the midst of maggots.
But sickness can creep as well as fly
and his both crept and flew,
drink stealing his brain.
He had started to drink heavily in the Corps
because booze would magic away his thoughts.
Then he drank on through and after college
until booze magicked away his thinking,
when he started to disremember what day it was,
or what month, or what year,
though he knew it was not wartime any more.
Huckstering his own mind,

he told himself that drinking diminished his
   burden,
and for awhile it did.
But with its diminishment,
he became his burden
and started to diminish.
One day, in his home in Vietnam, Virginia,
he asked himself, "Am I who I am? or am I some-
   one else?"
Like him, his nerves were shot,
for he was carrying in pieces
broken memories of the five years
since getting back from his year in Nam.
Once he looked at his eyes
in a mirror whose eyes looked back
like blood clots in his d.t.'s V.C.,
and he stood, unlike his mirror, cracked
and on the screaming side of sanity.
He was self-admitted to a veterans' hospital
because, at twenty-seven years of age,
he knew he would have to stay a year.
And so, dry and sane without booze
when he was twenty-eight years old,
he had peace.

Private First Class Oran Brodsky, U.S.M.C.

When the North Vietnamese opened up on the
    patrol
he was cut off and ran as far as he could
into what he knew would be a good cover
when an incoming tank shell came down right on
    top of him.
He was needlessly alive and knew it.
Except for one arm, he was unable to move,
and knew that, too.
He knew he lay in a heavy cluster of thick bush
and tall grass and taller trees,
and that this spot lay at the foot of some small
    hills,
and that beyond the small hills stood the great
    mountains.
He knew the land on which he lay dying
ran uneven and brilliant with colors.
The great mountains were black, the small hills
    brown,
and the land was shades and shadows
of greens and purples and yellows and reds
of flowers and weeds and strange shrubs

---

that grew as lovely as a man's life,
older and younger both and at once.
With his one good arm
he removed his dog tags
and flung them as far as he could
into the tall grass.
He knew he would probably never be found,
but that if he was, would probably be beyond
  identification.
So he lay there and waited for the evening to
  come,
for with the evening came the shadows,
and the evening and the shadows came,
and he felt them eat his feet and legs,
his trunk and chest, his arms and shoulders,
and finally his face and head.
And then he felt himself shadow
and become the evening and the earth of Vietnam.

Corporal Dudley Woodruff, U.S.M.C.

He will swear forever
that it was part of the Communist World-
    Conspiracy.
He spent a thirteen-month regular tour
in Vietnam as a clerk.
Upon completion of his thirteenth month, in June,
he was sent home to San Francisco,
where he reenlisted.
He got his Corporal's stripes, bonus money,
and his choice of a new duty station.
He chose Hawaii,
and after he had been in San Francisco a whole
    week,
he got his shipping-out orders
back to Vietnam.
He returned to Nam as a grunt,
and for the next several months
wrote seven hundred and fifty-six letters
to the Commandant of the Marine Corps,
his Senator, his Congressman,
and his Commander-in-Chief, the President.
He explained to each of them
that there had been a gross mistake

and he asked them to please help him,
and when they could, to kindly reply.
One day in June
he received four official letters:
one from the Commandant,
one from his Senator,
one from his Congressman,
and one from the President.
Each official said
that the government and the military Officially
    Apologized
and that both of them hoped such a silly, sad
    mistake
would never happen again,
and that the Corporal would be going home in
    July,
his present tour's thirteenth month.

Lance Corporal Jyo Mitshibutzi, U.S.M.C.

The napalm was dropped too close
and he caught fire and ran in a scream
until his squad Sergeant caught him
and knocked him down.
It took place in the evening
and the night took days to pass.
The whole enduring world was absolute rain.
A helicopter could not fly in
to take him out.
His uniform was burned
into the ragged raws of his flesh.
The medics could do nothing,
so his pain kept screaming to his pain.
His face was gone
but he could still speak.
He laughed, dying, saying,
"My eyes aren't slanted any more, man.
How about that?"

Private Richardo Carreras, U.S.M.C.

His wife told the prison psychiatrist
that ever since his return from Vietnam
he would sit up in bed all through the night
and stare back at the silence,
seeing, he told her, thousands of tracer shells
as they streaked screamless through their bedroom
and into the night's blackness.
His days became gouged by his nights
and his nights by screamless streaks
that trolled and tricked his brain and kept him
    awake.
Because he could not rest
he went through his days with darting, war-
    wrought eyes
that kept searching for the unseeable.
On the day of the truce,
he took her to a restaurant to celebrate.
When the waiter came upon them
like a moving, silent shadow,
her husband dropped his napkin, turned,
and smashed the waiter in the face,
sending the bones of his nose up into his brain,
and as the waiter fell,
her husband kicked in the back of his skull.

Everyone ran, screaming,
while her husband turned back around
and drank his coffee.
When the police arrived, she ran to them
and explained about her husband.
One of the policemen was a former Marine
who had also been a grunt in Nam.
He told the others to stay back,
then went into the restaurant alone.
Her husband looked up, saw him, and said nothing,
but he watched while the policeman came to stand
   in front of him
and take off his holster, and put it down.
Then the policeman slowly walked toward him,
making no quick, strange moves.
Her husband motioned for him to sit down.
The policeman sat down and quietly asked the
   ex-Private
why he killed the waiter.
Her husband replied, "Because,"
because that had been the answer given to him
for all of his other killing.

Corporal Jessesseppe Quinnpiac, U.S.M.C.

He cursed the dead their stench
since he was often ordered
to be with us on the Body Search Squad.
It was the squad's duty
to try and find American corpses
or to try and piece together
a reasonable facsimile.
What with the rats, and maggots, and heat,
it was an unpleasant detail
because we had to bag and tag the bodies
so that they could be shipped stateside for burial.
We were about a hundred feet from him,
lifting corpses aboard a helicopter,
when a booby trap
that had been attached to a blown-away leg
went off beneath him.
We heard the blast and saw him fly up,
separate into thousands,
and become air.
And then we were breathing him.

Sergeant Buford Joyce, U.S.M.C.

He killed the PFC and the Corporal,
blowing them both away
with a burst he heard
for a long time
until he did not hear it any more.
He came upon them
just as they were finishing with her.
She was twelve or thirteen,
but a Viet Cong,
and she had dropped her jammed weapon, an
    AK47,
that lay at his feet where he crept up,
having heard her screams.
The PFC was sitting on her head
and holding down her arms.
The Corporal was laughing
and between her legs.
The Sergeant bent down, picking up her weapon.
He unjammed it just as they were getting
up and off and out of her,
turning toward him.
He cut them both nearly in two,
emptying the whole clip,
firing at crotches and heading toward heads.

Then he went over to the girl,
aimed away her automatic,
and released the empty clip.
He placed the dead weapon beside her,
sat down and waited.
They found them like that,
and handed her over to the South Vietnamese,
who thought she had killed the two dead
    Americans.
The South Vietnamese, knowing the Cong,
did with her whatever they did with V.C.
before putting her in a tiger cage outside of
    Saigon.
After the sweeping operation was finished,
the Sergeant found out where they had taken the
    girl
and went to see her.
He spoke some broken Vietnamese
and asked her if she had told them
about what really had happened.
She said yes but that no one believed her.
Then she spat in his face,
saying she wished he had killed her, too.

The Sergeant left and went on for three more
   months,
trying to rest, day or night,
but could not sleep from thinking.
Finally there came to him at night
something that was a haunt to him.
He would not close his eyes
unless there was a light near by.
And then the haunt started to push itself into the
   day,
for just as he did not slay the raped,
neither could he slay the dead.
He committed suicide with a grenade one night
while standing guard duty.
The whole company started shooting,
killing the night and the bush,
thinking they were back.

Second Lieutenant Parvin Zelmer, U.S.M.C.

The reason he died?
He and the platoon came upon
three Vietnamese children, ages three, five, and eight,
who were playing with some tied-together pieces
of nice, shiny plastic that they had found in the grass.
The Lieutenant stood still
but ordered the rest of the platoon to fall back.
Then he asked the kids to put their toy,
a double booby trap, down gently,
but they did not understand
and pitched it to him,
and it bounced once and went boom,
gutting all four of them to shredded death.
A Congressman, upon hearing of the incident
from a news reporter,
asked the reporter one question:
"Was the booby-trap theirs or ours?"
And his question was the answer.

Corporal Pasquale Zumatte, U.S.M.C.

This village he now walked through
had been caught between a cross fire,
and only a few of its children were left alive.
He watched with careful eyes
the carefully watching eyes of the children
who looked at him but did not see him,
and who saw instead a man with a gun.
By the look on their death-breathing faces,
he could tell that it bereaved their lives
to be merely alive
while their parents were merely dead.
He went into a hut
to search and possibly destroy
but saw the destruction was already done.
There lay two men and a woman, dead.
A boy, six or seven years old,
had followed him through the door of the hut.
The PFC turned around and looked at the child,
then back to the bodies, knowing that two of the
    dead
were the child's parents,
now fly-swimming and green-tinged and stinking.
The PFC knelt to the boy

and put his arms out and brought the child close
now that war had said to him,
"Be your own mother. Be your own father.
The Marines killed her. The Viet Cong killed
    him."
Then the PFC held the boy back
and reached into his flak-jacket for some candy.
And the child reached behind his own back,
    paused, smiled,
then hurried a bayonet out from behind his back
and gutted the PFC's belly.
The Marine sat back and simply tumbled over,
    dead,
beside the stabbed and fallen corpse of the third
    dead adult,
a Viet Cong soldier who lay with some candy in
    his hands.

Private Cincinnatus Osgood, U.S.M.C.

He was a Teaching Fellow in a medical school
and had just received his Ph.D. in Bio-Anatomy
when he was drafted into the Marine Corps
where he was called Private Doctor
by his D.I.
who kept asking him
what was a physician doing in boot camp.
The Private had the highest intelligence rating
ever recorded on Parris Island.
Therefore, the Marine Corps made him a grunt.
He was sent to Vietnam,
and when a Major in Da Nang came across his
    records,
the Major asked him
if he would like to return home and go to O.C.S.
The Private Doctor told him no
and that he hated officers
and that he did not want to go home.
The Major thought him insane
and sent him to a naval psychiatrist aboard base.
The psychiatrist had been one of his students
in medical school, and told the Private Doctor
that he would be shipped back home immediately,
but he screamed no at the psychiatrist,

and said he thought the war experience was
  educational,
which made the psychiatrist think
that the Private Doctor was sick,
so the psychiatrist sent him to the base mental
  hospital
where he escaped and returned to his platoon.
They caught up with him,
but his Sergeant explained to them
that the man wasn't nuts,
saying to them that combat, and only combat,
would give the Private Doctor
the opportunity to make at least Lance Corporal,
so that no one could call him Private Doctor
  any more.

Lance Corporal Adam Worth, U.S.M.C.

It is a dead past but his mind cannot bury it,
so he laughs now with wounded laughter,
and retrospects about the future.
Since Hue and the Citadel,
his shell-shocked time
stretches between the seconds
and stands still to spite him.
All day, each day,
he sits on a bench
on the gentle rolling grounds
of Bethesda Naval Hospital,
thinking,
"Tomorrow it will be over,"
and tomorrow it is over,
over and over and over.
He talks to the grass and flowers
a strange, protective talk.
"Shhh," he says.
"Keep your colors soft and muted.
Hold back your blades until they are needed."

Lance Corporal Henry Hart, U.S.M.C.

Perhaps the guilt of war can be explained by all
  people,
but perhaps the meaning of the guilt only by their
  poets.
Had he made it through the war
he wanted to find words
and the good way with words
that he might write
in lovely, lasting words
what war had done to men.
Such matters as why a falling leaf
might make some men jump in terror,
and how never again would such men
truly trust shadows and silences.
A PFC who lay next to the Lance Corporal
said that while they waited
back on the ground,
the Lance Corporal kept quoting poets:
Robert Bly and Denise Levertov at first,
and then, once up in the air,
he went into the poems
of Robert Lowell and Erica Jong.
By the time the helicopter touched earth again,
the Lance Corporal was raving the words

of William Stafford and James Dickey
into the writings of Gary Snyder and Peter
    Davidson,
garbling them all up together
in a morphined babbling of beyond-morphine
    pain.
The PFC said the Lance Corporal
suddenly became still and said, "Words,"
and that then his eyes
just went looking forward forever,
toward nothing.

Corporal Ulysses Oznos, U.S.M.C.

His last day ran slowly
but lasted him his last day.
He was flown straight from Vietnam
to San Diego's veterans' hospital
during the same night he was blown away by a
   grenade.
When the doctors did what they could do,
and saw that it was not enough,
they had his parents flown in from his home town
to be with him those moments
to help him wait the long hours through.
Shed of his fear and shut of his hatred,
he was awake and aware and he could speak.
He spoke twice before he died.
He told his parents
there were young men who would never be old
and there were old men who had never been
   young.
Then he said he was tired of waiting
for the night to come and put the day to sleep.
He sat up in his bed,
reached up his hands as high as they would go,
and then quietly and slowly he lay back
and pulled down the sun.

Gunnery Sergeant Wayne Boone, U.S.M.C.

Oklahoma is the state
where every other corrupt politician
calls John Steinbeck a sonofabitch
and where, as every Okie knows,
every other sonofabitch
is a corrupt politician.
The Gunny will know that forever,
raised as he was in Oklahoma's dust
during the Depression.
He joined the Marines right before Korea,
and won his first stripe at the frozen Chosen.
After that war was quits,
he re-upped to proudly career the Corps.
Since then, until now, it had been Do This,
and his attitude was always Yes, Sir,
because the Gunny was all Marine and Duty.
But this war was something else.
He knew what was wrong about it,
but couldn't, even after three tours,
figure out what was right.
The Colonel agreed with him
that the politicians, theirs and ours,
were beyond understanding.

It was impossible to guess
which was more stupid about them:
their ignorance or their learning.
It seemed they were trying to stretch this one out
    forever,
all of them acting
like they were all the Fourth Person of the Holy
    Quadrangle.
Sweet Jesus H. God,
the Gunny said he would give half his stripes
and his left nut
to pitch a platoon of Senators and Congressmen
and the President as point man
against a platoon of Commissars and Peoples'
    Directors
and their Premier as point.
No one would win and they would all lose,
shooting up their own fool selves
much less the leftover crazies on the opposite side.
Hell: all his stripes and both nuts.

Lance Corporal Updike Fellows, U.S.M.C.

It was a sight better than doing nothing,
selling newspapers for the last year
ever since he got his discharge
and got out of the Marine Corps.
He had tried to get a better job,
but all his trying came to grief.
He went from this employer to that,
sick of his own smile, smiling
at the piety of the understanding faces
who kept telling him
that they indeed understood
but that he lacked the necessary education,
the business experience,
and that there was no need for his talents
with a grenade launcher
or his ability to survive in the jungle
or his prowess at karate.
So he started to sell newspapers
and kept trying
and kept failing
to find a better job.
At the end of a year,

he returned to the Marine Corps and reenlisted,
and got back his uniform, his medals, and his
    manhood.
He and the Sergeant Recruiter who signed him up
    again
talked a good long while about the Old Corps,
and they exchanged wounded war stories and
    defeated jokes.
Finally the new Lance Corporal had to leave.
He said he was sick
about the way the war had been fought
and was just as sick
about the way the war had not been fought.
The Sergeant Recruiter watched him leave,
and said to him not to be too discouraged,
and yelled out to the disappearing Lance Corporal,
"The next time, Marine. The next time."

Chief Petty Officer Elijah Christian, Corpsman, U.S.N.

He used to measure his sanity by how much he
    forgot,
and though nothing is that was
of the beyond-repairs of his wound-bearing past,
some of his memories were deathless,
and he could not kill them.
The memories were heavy, and their heaviness
    dark,
yet when the former medic remembered the war,
he always remembered how forgettable war really
    was.
When he would least suspect it,
his memory would battle with his trying to recall
the Marines of the platoon
to which he had been assigned:
their names, their faces,
how they managed to live, and how they died.
He would be at work,
or making love to his wife,
or walking down the street,
or playing with his son,
when out of the heavy darkness of his past

skeletal fingers would reach forth from back there
to touch his thinking,
conjuring up the living and the dead,
the meaning and the meaninglessness of war.
Then he would be unable to talk about Vietnam
or unable to talk about anything else except
    Vietnam,
as if time had not melted his rage
but had frozen it.
He knew that someday,
in the tomorrows after tomorrow,
he would come to disremember
the little that he could truly recall.
Today, in this February of 1976,
more than two years
after the truce was signed,
he received a telephone call
from an ex-Private he had saved in Nam,
a double-amputee who stepped on a land mine
and who said that afterward,
while he lay still,
he had listened to his blown-off legs get up
    without him
and slowly walk away.
The ex-Private had been flown Med-Evac from
    Nam to San Diego,

where what was left of his charred stumps
had gangrened and so were amputated further
so that, from the waist down,
he simply wasn't any more.
The ex-Private had then been flown
to Bethesda Naval Hospital
for long-range rehabilitation.
The former medic was from Washington, D.C.,
and when he was discharged,
returned to his home
and started in college at American University.
He heard from a buddy, who also lived in
    Washington
and with whom he had served in Nam,
that the ex-Private was out in Maryland in
    Bethesda,
only a few miles from where the ex-medic lived,
and so he went to visit him several times
at the hospital that first year, 1971.
But for almost four years now
he had not made a visit
because it took him days to get over it.
When he got the telephone call today,
the ex-Private told him
that he was getting out of rehabilitation
and was going home.

They agreed to get together for a beer or two
to celebrate the occasion.
They met at a bar in Georgetown
and they had their beer, then several more beers,
talking about politics and college and jobs
and about everything, except the war.
By the time the day ended,
they were both three sheets to the wind drunk.
He shook hands with the ex-Private
and then stood watching in the old renewed awe
as the double-amputee walked away
with only a touch of a tilt
that only the knowing would recognize and realize
that this was a man who was half plastic and
metal
from his navel down.
Then the former medic went to his car
and drove away, and he noticed that it might rain.
And when he noticed, he recalled the Vietnam
monsoons,
and suddenly he realized that not once
had the war even been mentioned that day,
the two of them having carefully avoided the
subject
all through those beers, all day long,
and now he realized
that because Vietnam had never been brought up,

it was really the only subject they had talked
    about.
He drove on around and through the city,
driving past the Washington Monument,
the Jefferson Memorial,
Lincoln,
the White House,
and finally found himself
driving up the circular street
that led to the Capitol building.
And when he came to the front
of the Capitol of the United States of America,
he stopped his car and got out.
He stood and looked up,
up at the tall dome
and up to the waving flag atop the Capitol
and beyond the flag, the sky
with its clouds yet to rain, its thunders yet to fall,
and he came to attention, saluted,
and screamed an animal howl of a scream
whose echo backed its echo
in a cry calling to many cries:
Why?
Why?
Why?
Why?